I0418644

5 CATEGORIES OF SELF-CARE

THE ULTIMATE GUIDE TO FINDING SELF-LOVE AND HAPPINESS

KATHERINE IBARRA

This guidebook is dedicated to the loving memory of my mom, Jeanelle Stovall, and my Godmother, Katherine Dunham. Both of these incredible women ingrained in me the teachings of self-love, compassion, and humility. I also want to dedicate this book to my ever-loving and supportive husband, Nathan, and to my two beautiful daughters, Isabella and Celeste, who are my biggest fans and inspire me to keep reaching for the stars daily.

CONTENTS

INTRODUCTION

Do you feel unhealthy and unfit? Do you look in the mirror and not like what you see? Do you talk about problems in a healthy way and ask for help when needed? Do you spend time with toxic people, or do you have meaningful and more intimate experiences with others? Do you carve out time to reflect on yourself and what is meaningful? Are you unable to figure out your direction? Are you close to burnout at work or school and find yourself paralyzed and going nowhere fast?

This guidebook empowers you to regain your life and feel more in control of your destiny.

In the 5 Categories of Self-Care book, licensed Clinical Therapist Katherine Ibarra encourages the reader to dig deeper and reflect on how much or how little they care for themselves in 5 different areas of self-care. Mrs. Ibarra's approach is patient-centered and will ask the reader to complete   Physical,   Psychological/Emotional,   Social,

Spiritual, and Professional self-care assessments. The reader will then need to identify areas they wish to improve on and begin to focus on incorporating new healthy habits into everyday routines. These assessments and techniques are practical and grounded in clinical practice and research.

Hi, I am Katherine Ibarra, and my approach to therapy combines Positive Psychology, Cognitive Behavioral Therapy, Motivational Interviewing, Psychodynamic therapy, Narrative therapy, Mindfulness practices, Forgiveness Therapy, and Solution-Focused Therapy. I have over 16 years of experience working with adult patients with relationship issues, depression, financial stressors, anxiety, parenting problems, career challenges, ADHD, grief, life transitions, self-esteem issues, stress, trauma, post-traumatic stress disorder, women's issues, multicultural concerns, and more. I am passionate about helping individuals, couples, families, and friends navigate various unique complexities of issues to build stronger, healthier relationships with themselves and others.

Readers need to be open and willing to do the work. They must be committed to loving themselves and finding true happiness. Patients of mine from all walks of life and at various stages in life have been most successful in significantly improving their mental health by being active participants and completing the "homework" I assign them.

This guidebook will include the 5 Self-Care assessments. Readers are to actively participate and be completely honest in their self-assessment of areas they are doing well in and areas they wish to improve and write them down in a journal or notebook. There is no right or wrong way of answering assessments.

If you are fully committed to learning from this guide, you will also successfully maintain healthy levels of self-care. It will be empowering and life-changing.

PHYSICAL SELF-CARE

Over 1,000 studies examined by the John W. Brick Foundation found that 89% showed significant proof that physical activity positively impacts mental health. Physical self-care also includes eating healthy and regularly, getting regular check-ups with the doctor or specialty medical provider, maintaining personal hygiene, wearing clothes that make you feel good about yourself, and having good sleep patterns.

Through the physical self-care assessment, you will identify areas of physical self-care you wish to improve and barriers and brainstorm ways to overcome them.

1.1 PHYSICAL SELF-CARE ASSESSMENT

- Do I have a healthy food intake and a good relationship with food?
- Do I have good personal hygiene and keep my external body clean?
- Do I exercise consistently?
- Do I wear clothes that help me feel good about myself?
- Do I eat Regularly?
- Do I participate in fun activities such as hiking, walking, rock climbing, dancing, sports, and eating out?
- Do I sleep through the night?
- Make the bed in the mornings?
- Do I attend preventative medical appointments, such as annual check-ups with doctor/specialty medical providers or dentists?
- Do I rest when I am sick, or do I never rest?

- **Overall, how am I doing with physical self-care?**

1.2 TYING IN HEALTHY NEW HABITS

Now, review the top area(s) you wish to improve in physical self-care. Let's say, for example, you want to improve your exercise.

Looking at a typical week for you, what could be a realistic, healthy new goal to incorporate into your regular routines?

"Maybe I could wake up 30 minutes earlier on Mondays and Wednesdays and jump on the Peloton? Or do a 15-30 minute mini cardio workout? Then get in the shower and get ready for the day?"

How you incorporate new healthy habits is entirely up to you, but schedule yourself in a calendar, set reminders, and time yourself until it becomes a very natural habit. This is similar to Pavlov's dog Theory of classical conditioning.

Then imagine, "If I stay consistent with my plan, I will feel in better shape, have more energy, be more productive, and feel better about myself."

PSYCHOLOGICAL/EMOTIONAL SELF CARE

D o you have unrealistically high standards of self, consistently feel out of place or unworthy, only focus on negative feedback, and have difficulty accepting compliments? Do you often experience self-defeating thoughts? Do you have difficulty expressing your feelings?

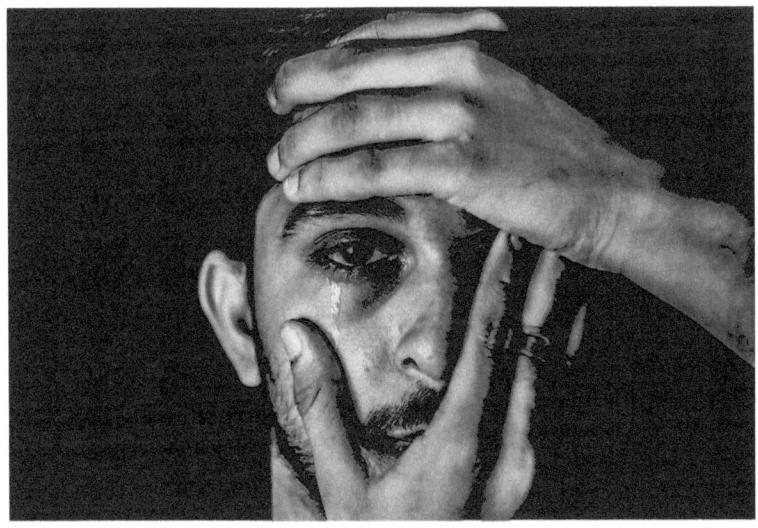

Through the Psychological/Emotional self-care assessment, you will identify areas of emotional self-care you wish to improve and brainstorm ways to overcome certain barriers.

2.1 PSYCHOLOGICAL/EMOTIONAL SELF-CARE ASSESSMENT

- Do I recognize my own strengths and achievements and am able to take compliments?
- Do I participate in hobbies that I enjoy ....ie Pickle ball, knitting, crochet, reading, cooking?
- Do I get off the grid...ie put the phone on airplane mode, shutdown computer and not scroll through social media platforms?
- Do I learn new things unrelated to work or school that I enjoy?
- Do I take time off from work when needed....ie actually using a personal day?
- Do I express my feelings in a healthy way....ie talk to friends, journal, talk to a therapist?
- Do I go on vacations or day trips regularly?
- Do I do something comforting, such as Snuggling on a couch and watching a favorite movie, taking a long bath or spa treatment, or relaxing in the hot tub outside during the winter?
- Do I find humor in life?

- **Overall, how am I doing with my psychological and emotional self-care?**

2.2 STRENGTHS USE PLAN

I want you to complete a Strengths Use plan for the next week or so. This is one of my go-to first assignments for patients. Everyone has strengths, but those who are more mindful of their strengths are more confident, less stressed, and have stable moods.

In the Strengths use plan, I want you to intentionally and purposely use one strength in either new or familiar ways every day for one week.

Here provided is a list of strengths to review and consider utilizing:

- Kindness
- Love
- Flexibility
- Gratitude
- Humility
- Honesty
- Social Awareness
- Humor
- Self Regulation
- Persistence
- Enthusiasm
- Love of Learning
- Hope
- Leadership
- Spirituality
- Appreciation of Beauty
- Teamwork

- Creativity
- Analytical
- Forgiveness
- Optimism

Now, write it down in a notebook for one through seven days. Next to each day, I want you to write down a strength and a plan.

Three examples:

- **Day 1: Strength:** Kindness * **Plan:** Give a compliment to the barista
- **Day 2: Strength:** Love of Learning * **Plan:** Will sign-up for a cooking class
- **Day 3: Strength:** Gratitude * **Plan:** Will text friend & say "I love you!"

2.3 DISTORTED THINKING

Regarding your Psychological/emotional self-care, I feel it is also crucial that you assess for any "Cognitive Distortions" and process how to overcome those distortions.

In Cognitive Therapy, the main concept is that our thoughts significantly influence our emotions. Those thoughts can positively or negatively affect how we interact with others and view certain experiences. Psychiatrist David Burns has coined the term "Cognitive Distortions," which are negative ways of thinking that start to become habits, so you don't even realize they are happening.

Reflecting on your own experiences of negative thinking, have you experienced a sense of inferiority, shame, worthlessness, or that the worst possible outcomes will come true? In what ways could you counter those distortions and re-frame a thought to make it more positive?

Quick Tip Ideas to Help You Reframe:

- **Using Putting Thoughts On Trial Technique**: Write down that negative thought. Then imagine being a defense attorney and prosecutor who needs to provide actual evidence that supports that thought or goes against it. The evidence cannot be based on assumptions or predictions. Then, as objectively as possible, as a judge, you are to decide if this thought was rational or irrational and what could be a more positive spin to the thought. This technique effectively slows your brain from spiraling and significantly decreases the impulse to make irrational decisions based on irrational thought processes.

- **Best Case, Likely, And Worst Case Scenario**: Write down all 3 case scenarios you are considering. Acknowledge them but do your best to focus time and energy only on the likely case scenarios. Again, you acknowledge your thoughts but redirect away from the hyper-fixation, time, and energy on the worst-case scenario that will never actually happen.

2.4 HEALTHY VS. UNHEALTHY COPING STRATEGIES

Coping strategies: In life, we acquire conscious and unconscious coping strategies to deal with stressors, problems, and uncomfortable emotions. Unhealthy coping strategies give us instant gratification but lead to long-term consequences. Healthy coping strategies, on the other hand, may not give you instant gratification but will lead to long-term benefits.

Examples of Unhealthy Coping Strategies:

- Projection
- Emotional eating
- Procrastination
- Rumination
- Victim-mentality
- Drug or Alcohol abuse
- Social isolation
- Self-harm
- Aggression

Examples of Healthy Coping Strategies:

- Self-Comforting
- Talking about problems and asking for help
- Healthy eating
- Seeking professional help
- Relaxation techniques (i.e., using mindfulness practices and deep breathing)

- Problem-solving

Example #1 Scenario of Unhealthy Coping Strategies:

Grace is upset with her boss because she feels she has not been given equal growth opportunities. Instead of talking with her boss, she has a growing sense of resentment. Grace has learned that she can suppress that anger and feelings of being a victim by *drinking alcohol* after work when she comes home. Drinking masks that feeling of contempt for her boss at that moment, but her resentment only continues to grow and fester every time she goes back to work.

What are the possible consequences of these unhealthy coping strategies?

Grace will become increasingly dependent on alcohol to manage her negative emotions and will start feeling that she needs to drink on the job to get through the workday. The quality of her work will be negatively impacted, and once her boss becomes aware that she is under the influence while working, she will most likely be let go.

What are some possible healthy coping strategies for Grace?

Grace could start going to kickboxing classes after work instead of drinking to blow off steam. She could talk to friends, family, or a therapist and, in a healthy way, talk about her feelings. Then, she could ask her boss if they could speak at work. Grace assertively could say: "I was hoping for that promotion opportunity at work. Could you provide me feedback on ways to take more initiative and discuss a growth plan with earmarks?" The boss may be receptive and supportive in helping her grow in the company and get that promotion or raise. If the boss, on the other hand, is not receptive and is very dismissive, then Grace needs to review her Spiritual Self-Care *(Further discussed in Chapter 4) and* Professional Self-Care *(Further discussed in Chapter 5)*. She needs to take some time to reflect on her current work environment and ask herself if this company or even line of work is the right fit for her. Perhaps this is a pivotal moment for Grace, where she decides that her company is holding her back from success and happiness, and she needs to make a change by applying to other jobs and networking. I always say that everything happens for a reason. Sometimes, we go through situations that are not good, so we appreciate and get excited about the good situations when they do come. Note: Grace, though, should not resign from her current job until she gets a new one. Unless she can financially stay afloat for at least 6 months, she should take that time to brainstorm on career goals and careers.

What are my Unhealthy Coping Strategies?

Write in your journal:

1. What is a problem I am currently experiencing?
2. What are my typical unhealthy coping strategies?
3. What have been the consequences of my unhealthy coping strategies in the past?

What are my Healthy Coping Strategies?

1. What are some healthier coping strategies I can use?
2. What could be some positive outcomes from these healthier coping strategies?
3. What are my barriers to using healthy coping strategies?

SOCIAL SELF-CARE

Do you find that you are around toxic or hostile environments in work settings, friendships, and family, or do you surround yourself with individuals you can trust and who love and support you unconditionally? Do you find that you can have meaningful connections with people, or do you find it challenging to make those connections?

Through the Social self-care assessment, you will identify areas of Social self-care you wish to improve and brainstorm ways to overcome specific barriers.

3.1 SOCIAL SELF-CARE ASSESSMENT

- Do I call or write to friends/family who are far away?
- Do I regularly spend time with family who are local? Ie. Taco Tuesday nights, Sunday dinners.
- Do I spend time with people who I like?
- Do I do enjoyable activities with other people?
- Do I have stimulating conversations with other people?
- Do I meet new people and enjoy getting to know them?
- Do I ask others for help when needed?
- Do I spend time alone with my romantic partner (if applicable)?
- Do I have intimate time with my romantic partner (if applicable)?

- **Overall, how am I doing with social self-care?**

3.2 ASSESSING YOUR SOCIAL CIRCLES

Sometimes, writing gratitude letters or gratitude journals regarding a loved one helps give you insight. If you find yourself quickly being able to answer the following prompts regarding a loved one, they are most likely very loving and supportive, and you are happy when you are around them. Spend more time with these people. If you have difficulty answering the following prompts, you must ask yourself: Are these individuals the best for me right now in my life? Are they toxic and very negative? Do you feel drained, sad, or angry around these people? If so, spend less time with these individuals.

Gratitude Prompts to write in a journal:

I was happy when my (blank) did......

The best part of time we spent together was....

Something good my (blank) did was.....

My (blank) made me laugh when......

I was grateful for my (blank) when.....

Something my (blank) accomplished was....

My (blank) helped me when....

A challenge my (blank) overcame was....

I noticed one of my (blank's) strengths when....

I was impressed when my (blank) did....

Something memorable my (blank) and I did was....

Something fun my (blank) and I did together was....

I felt admiration toward my (blank) when....

Three Forms of Communication

Now, I will review three common forms of communication. I need you to identify and acknowledge your communication style in different settings, including family, friends, work/supervisors/co-workers, and significant others.

Passive Communicator: These individuals tend to be people-pleasers and have great difficulty expressing their thoughts and feelings effectively. Many times, even well-meaning people who are unaware of the passive communicator's needs and wants take advantage of them.

Common traits of passive communicators include:

- Bashful
- Frequently apologizes
- Prioritizes the needs of others
- Makes poor eye contact
- Does not express wants/needs
- Lacks confidence

Aggressive Communicator: An individual will express that only their needs, wants, and feelings matter and will ignore the needs and wants of others.

Common traits of Aggressive communicators include:

- Difficulty managing anger
- Puts down others, insults, and dominates
- Raises voice often
- Unwilling to compromise

- Overtly is hostile
- Deliberately hurts others

Assertive Communicator: This form of communication is the most ideal in any setting. Whether with family, friends, coworkers, or significant others, assertive communication emphasizes the importance of both people's needs. An assertive communicator respects self and the other party, and they can clearly state their needs, wants, and feelings, but they must also be able to listen and respect the needs of others. Assertive communicators have confidence and are willing to find compromise and or offer solution-focused ideas.

Common traits of Assertive communicators include:

- Thoughtful and listens
- Clearly states needs and wants
- Confident tone/body language
- Willing to compromise, shows compassion
- Stands up for self
- Makes good eye contact

Example Scenario Using All Three Types of Communication:

Scenario: Your boss needs to have a sense of time boundaries and never seems to be mindful when it is the end of a work day. This boss has a habit of always asking you to stay late and work on a project that will take an additional 2 hours to complete.

Passive Response: "Sure, I will stay late and work on the project." (Your internal monologue, though, is saying, "I cannot believe my boss asked me to stay late again. Now, I need to cancel my plans. I can't stand my boss. I need to quit one of these days!!")

Aggressive Response: "Are you out of your mind? You always ask me to stay late. Ask someone else!"

Assertive Response: "I have plans tonight; however, I would be happy to help with the project during my working hours tomorrow."

Do you see how the assertive communicator respects self and boss, states needs and wants, and presents compromise? That assertive communicator states the need to leave work on time so they can do meaningful activities outside of work. That assertive communicator establishes healthy boundaries supporting work and personal life balance. Honestly, most bosses really appreciate an assertive communicator because they know exactly what their employee's needs and wants are, including the need for professional/personal life balance. That boss will respect that employee and now only ask that employee to work on projects within that employee's working hours. Now, I realize that there are bad bosses who are self-absorbed and critical. Still, there are more good bosses who understand that as long as they can support that balance for their employees, those employees will be more productive and happier and will not up and quit or be aggressive in communication.

Now, the mission, if you choose to accept it, is to be much more intentional and mindful of always practicing assertive communication in every setting of your life. Respectfully express your needs and wants, and find compromise or offer solution-focused ideas.

3.3 PERSONAL BOUNDARIES

Another essential part of social self-care is knowing your boundaries to be clear in your assertive communication. Personal boundaries are the limits and rules we set for ourselves in relationships. People with healthy boundaries do not compromise their values and morals and are independent in their own opinions. A person who is very dependent on the opinion of others and fears rejection if they do not comply is said to have Porous boundaries. A person who always keeps others at a distance and avoids intimacy/close relationships is said to have Rigid boundaries.

Common Traits For Rigid Boundaries Include But Not Limited To:

- Difficulty trusting or asking for help
- Avoids intimacy and close relationships
- Reluctant to show vulnerability
- Quick to cut people out of life
- Very protective of personal information
- May seem detached, even with romantic partners
- Keeps others at a distance to avoid being rejected

Common Traits For Porous Boundaries Include But Not Limited To:

- Craves external validation
- Overshares personal information
- Has difficulty saying "no" to the requests of others
- Over-involved in other people's dramas
- Dependent on the opinions of others
- Allows others to mistreat them
- Fears rejection if they do not comply with others

Common Traits For Healthy Boundaries Include But Not Limited To:

- Values own opinions
- Doesn't compromise values for others
- Shares personal information but doesn't over or under-share.
- Are very clear in verbalizing their wants and needs
- Can say "no" without feeling guilty

Now, most people have a mix of all three types of boundaries. You may have very porous boundaries with friends and family, rigid boundaries at work, and healthy boundaries with romantic relationships. Everyone is different, but it is important to know your personal boundaries in these various settings to feel more in control when navigating various relationships and settings.

You also want to consider your cultural background and learned behaviors from childhood, which may have influenced your personal boundaries in different settings and relationships.

Delving further into the types of boundaries, I will review Physical, Intellectual, Emotional, Sexual, Material, and Time boundaries.

Physical Boundaries: These relate to personal space and physical touch, as well as being aware of what is appropriate and what is not in various settings and types of relationships, such as shaking hands, hugging, and kissing. Physical boundaries can be violated when someone touches you when you don't want them to or if someone invades your personal space by going through your phone or other belongings.

Intellectual Boundaries: These boundaries involve respecting one's own and others' points of view and setting appropriate boundaries when one has opposing views. Should we talk about the weather or religion? Intellectual boundaries can be violated when someone quickly dismisses or belittles another person's thoughts or ideas.

Emotional Boundaries: These relate to a person's feelings. Similar to intellectual boundaries, emotional boundaries can be violated when someone quickly dismisses the emotions that you are expressing. "You're not sad; just get over it."

Sexual Boundaries: These relate to a person's emotional, intellectual, and physical aspects of sexuality. Healthy sexual boundaries are about knowing and understanding each other's wants, desires, and limitations. Sexual boundaries can be violated, though, with unwanted sexual advances, unwanted sexual touch, pressure to engage in sexual acts, and unwanted sexual comments.

Material Boundaries: This refers to money and material things. Healthy Material boundaries involve knowing your limits regarding sharing your things. You may not want to lend your car to someone you just met or to a family member who never refills the gas tank. Material boundaries are violated when someone damages your property, does not take care of it, or steals it.

Time Boundaries: This includes how you use and value your time. Healthy time boundaries require a good balance of time for work, relationships, hobbies, family, and friends. Time boundaries are violated, though, when someone has porous boundaries and feels forced to give all of their time to one person or an event.

SPIRITUAL SELF-CARE

C an you carve out time to take nature hikes or sit in a park and self-reflect? Can you stop and think about what is meaningful to you, what stimulates you, and what gives you purpose in life?

Through the Spiritual self-care assessment, you will identify areas of Spiritual self-care you wish to improve and brainstorm ways to overcome certain barriers.

4.1 SPIRITUAL SELF-CARE ASSESSMENT

- Do I recognize the things that give meaning to my life?
- Do I act in accordance with my morals and values?
- Do I spend time in nature or take a walk in the park?
- Do I meditate (If applicable)?
- Do I pray (If applicable)?
- Do I set aside time for thought and reflection?
- Do I participate in a cause that is important to me? Maybe I could find a 5K fundraiser that supports a cause that is very meaningful to me?
- Do I appreciate art that is thought provoking to me....ie through film, literature, music, architecture, photography?

- **Overall, how am I doing with Spiritual self-care?**

Now, with spiritual self-care, can you tie in that new healthy habit to your regular routines?

Example: "Maybe an hour before getting ready for bed, I can put my phone on airplane mode and reflect and journal about one positive experience I had during the day." You can also use Strengths use plan for this healthy new habit. Identify one strength that you utilized during the day. This helps you focus more on the positive experiences and your strengths vs. negative experiences and self-sabotaging thoughts.

4.2 NARRATIVE THERAPY FOR SPIRITUAL SELF-CARE

Writing about the past, present, and future life can be very cathartic and bring meaning and value to your experiences. It helps you to reflect, acknowledge growth, and identify lessons learned. Having that greater sense of self can contribute to great happiness and fulfillment.

The Past:

Write the story of your past. Be sure to talk about childhood, young adulthood, and challenges you faced and overcame by applying your strengths.

The Present:

Write about your life now. How are you different today than when you were your younger self? What are your current strengths, and what challenges are you facing?

The Future:

Write about your ideal future. What are your hopes and dreams? How do you think your future will be different from your present life?

5

PROFESSIONAL SELF-CARE

Most individuals work an average of 40-60 hours a week, depending on the type of job. That is a large portion of time in a person's life, so the hope is that you are in a career that you love and can find a healthy balance.

Be sure to always advocate for professional and personal life balance. Remember that with assertive communication, you respect yourself and other parties when communicating your needs/wants and finding compromise or presenting solution-focused ideas.

Through the Professional self-care assessment, you will identify areas of professional self-care you wish to improve and brainstorm ways to overcome certain barriers.

5.1 PROFESSIONAL SELF-CARE ASSESSMENT

- Do I delegate when needed?
- Do I say "no" to excessive new responsibilities and assert realistic goals?
- Do I take on projects that are interesting or rewarding and prioritize tasks?
- Do I learn new things related to my profession?
- Do I make time to talk and build relationships with colleagues?
- Do I take breaks during work, i.e., walk away from my workspace and take a walk or eat lunch?
- Do I keep healthy snacks nearby?
- Do I maintain a balance between my professional and personal life?

- Do I have an organized workspace that allows me to be more productive?
- Do I advocate for fair pay, benefits, and other needs?

- **Overall, how am I doing with Professional self-care?**

6

WHAT IS NEXT?

Now that you have identified areas that you wish to improve, you can start to plan the implementation of those healthier new habits and ways of thinking. Remember that this is not a race; change gradually occurs over time. Be realistic about short-term goals you can accomplish in a given week and be persistent in completing those short-term goals. Those short-term goals start adding up, and before you know it, you will achieve your long-term goals. Stay present, though, and stay focused, and change will happen.

Example of new healthy habits: "My night routine this week will involve writing one sentence in my journal about my strengths for the day and not looking at social media or my phone at least an hour before going to bed."

6.1 CREATING A FOCUS PLAN

- Identify healthy new habits you wish to incorporate and tie into daily routines.
- Pace yourself, and try not to be overly ambitious because that can lead to falling out of habit and being overwhelmed.
- Create a schedule with reminders, time yourself with new habits until it becomes very natural.
- Prepare for the task: Eliminate distractions, unavoidable distractions, physical preparation.
- Imagine the outcome.

CONCLUSION

I hope this book empowers you to be in the driver's seat of your life and feel fulfilled and confident. Continue to assess the 5 Categories of Self-Care and observe your progress and ability to maintain healthy levels. Once you can maintain healthy levels long-term, you will most likely be at the peak of your life and be happy with yourself. Sometimes, parts of our lives get neglected, but you can restore those areas to healthy levels again with some tender, loving care and intentional changes.

Now, for a little quiz to see what you choose in this Cognitive Model Practice exercise, I will give you a scenario where two different people experience the same situation; however, one individual has an irrational thought, and the other has a more rational thought.

Situation: Sara and Jeanelle both receive a negative evaluation at work.

*Sara's Reaction:

Sara immediately has a **negative/irrational thought**: "I'm such a loser; I will probably get fired because of this. My life is over."

Emotion: Depressed and Nervous

Behavior: Sara avoids her boss and continues to perform poorly. Her boss takes note of this continued poor performance and lack of initiative.

Outcome: Due to this lack of improvement, her boss does fire Sara.

*Jeanelle's Reaction:

On the other hand, Jeanelle is more rational: "Man, it is too bad I got a poor evaluation, but maybe there is a way to improve."

Emotion: Disappointed but Motivated.

Behavior: Jeanelle makes a point of following up with her boss and asking how she can improve and what a growth plan could look like. Jeanelle gradually improves, and her boss takes note of the significant progress.

Outcome: Jeanelle's boss acknowledges her incredible progress and gives her a promotion.

WHAT ARE YOUR TAKEAWAYS?

Remember that these two individuals experienced the same situation; however, because their thought processes differed, they had very different outcomes.

So, hopefully, you choose to think like Jeanelle, see the power in having a positive mindset, and apply your many strengths to steer your life in your chosen direction.

Remember that part of psychological/emotional self-care is healthily expressing feelings. If you need additional support in navigating life's various storms, I encourage you to contact a therapist. Zocdoc.com is an excellent resource for locating mental health providers in your area and your insurance network.

I want to express my gratitude for joining me in this guide-book and encourage you to continue referring to it throughout your life. I hope you embrace your self-love path with kindness, patience, and compassion. We all possess the strength and wisdom to cultivate a life filled with self-care and happiness.

If you found this book helpful, I would appreciate it if you left a favorable review for this book on Amazon!

REFERENCES AND RESOURCES

Therapy Worksheets | Therapist Aid. (n.d.). Therapist Aid. https://www.therapistaid.com/therapy-worksheets

Ihrsa. (2022b, April 29). *New Report: Exercise Plays Key Role in Mental Health & Well-being.* IHRSA. https://www.ihrsa.org/improve-your-club/new-report-exercise-plays-key-role-in-mental-health-well-being/#

MSEd, K. C. (2022, November 20). *Pavlov's Dogs and the Discovery of Classical Conditioning.* Verywell Mind. https://www.verywellmind.com/pavlovs-dogs-2794989

Kapil, R. (2022, March 14). *How and Why to Practice Self-care - Mental Health First Aid.* Mental Health First Aid. https://www.mentalhealthfirstaid.org/2022/03/how-and-why-to-practice-self-care/

Burns. (2020, January 9). *Secrets of Self-Esteem #2.* Feeling Good. https://feelinggood.com/2014/01/06/secrets-of-self-esteem-2-negative-and-positive-distortions/

NY Mental Health Center. (2024, November 19). *Katherine Ibarra Provider Bio Therapists.* https://nymentalhealthcenter.com/therapists/

ZocDoc. (n.d.). ZocDoc. https://www.zocdoc.com/